Sensational Human Body Science Projects

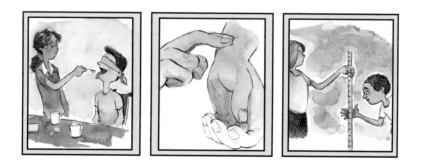

ANN BENBOW AND COLIN MABLY

ILLUSTRATIONS BY TOM LABAFF

Enslow Elementary

an imprint of

Enslow Publishers, Inc.

40 Industrial Road
Box 398
Berkeley Heights, NJ 07922
USA

http://www.enslow.com

Enslow Elementary, an imprint of Enslow Publishers, Inc.

Enslow Elementary® is a registered trademark of Enslow Publishers, Inc.

Library of Congress Cataloging-in-Publication Data

Benbow, Ann.
    Sensational human body science projects / Ann Benbow and Colin Mably.
      p. cm. — (Real life science experiments)
    Includes bibliographical references and index.
    Summary: "Presents several easy-to-do science experiments about senses and the human body"—Provided by publisher.
    ISBN-13: 978-0-7660-3149-4
    ISBN-10: 0-7660-3149-7
    1. Human physiology—Experiments—Juvenile literature. 2. Senses and sensation—Experiments—Juvenile literature. 3. Biology projects—Juvenile literature. I. Mably, Colin. II. Title.
    QP42.B378 2010
    612—dc22
                              2008023929

Printed in the United States of America

10 9 8 7 6 5 4 3 2 1

To Our Readers: We have done our best to make sure all Internet Addresses in this book were active and appropriate when we went to press. However, the authors and the publisher have no control over and assume no liability for the material available on those Internet sites or on other Web sites they may link to. Any comments or suggestions can be sent by e-mail to comments@enslow.com or to the address on the back cover.

♻ Enslow Publishers, Inc., is committed to printing our books on recycled paper. The paper in every book contains 10% to 30% post-consumer waste (PCW). The cover board on the outside of each book contains 100% PCW. Our goal is to do our part to help young people and the environment too!

Illustration Credits: Tom LaBaff

Photo Credits: Ashley Turner, p. 28; © Bela Tibor Kozma/iStockphoto.com, p. 24; Dreyer's/Edy's Grand Ice Cream, p. 16; Library of Congress, Prints & Photographs Division, p. 36; Shutterstock, pp. 8, 12, 40; © Steve Debenport/iStockphoto.com, p. 32; © Tracy Whiteside/iStockphoto.com, p. 44; WireImage/Getty Images, p. 20.

Cover Photo: Kristian Sekulic/istockphoto.com

Contents

Experiments with a 🎀 symbol feature **Ideas for Your Science Fair.**

Introduction

Human bodies are amazing. In many ways they are alike. Humans have eyes, ears, legs, arms, a nose, and a mouth. Humans are also different from each other. They can have different colors of skin, eyes, and hair. Some humans are tall and others are short.

Like many animals, humans have five senses: sight, hearing, touch, taste, and smell. They also have different levels of senses. Some people have very good sight, while others cannot see at all. When one sense does not work well, humans can become better at using other senses. People with deafness may have a better sense of smell. Those with poor sight can use their senses of touch and hearing better than most people.

You can use this book to investigate many things about the human body. You will be asking questions and doing experiments. By the end, you will know a lot more about the human body.

Science Fair Ideas

The investigations in this book will help you learn how to do experiments. After every investigation, you will find ideas for science fair projects. You may want to try one of these ideas, or you might think of a better project.

This book has a Learn More section. The books and Web sites in this section can give you more ideas for science fair projects.

Remember, science is all about asking questions. A science fair gives you the chance to investigate your own questions and record your results. It also lets you share your findings with your fellow scientists.

Safety First!

These are important rules to follow as you experiment.

1 Always have an adult nearby when doing experiments.

2 Follow instructions with care, especially safety warnings.

3 Never experiment with electrical outlets.

4 Use safety scissors, and have an adult handle any sharp objects.

5 Use only alcohol thermometers, never mercury!

6 Stay in a safe place if making outdoor observations.

7 Treat living things with care. Some may sting or be poisonous!

8 Keep your work area clean and organized.

9 Clean up and put materials away when you are done.

10 Always wash your hands when you are finished.

Experiment 1
How Well Can You Hear Soft Sounds?

Does your ability to hear change the farther you get from a sound? Write down your ideas and your reasons for them.

Now Let's Find Out!

1 Find a large space with a hard surface (like a driveway, garage, or patio). Starting at one end of the surface, put down a 10-meter (33½-foot) piece of masking tape. Use measuring tape and a marker to mark off every meter on the masking tape.

2 Turn your back to your partner. Keep your notebook and pen handy. Ask your partner to drop a penny one meter away from you.

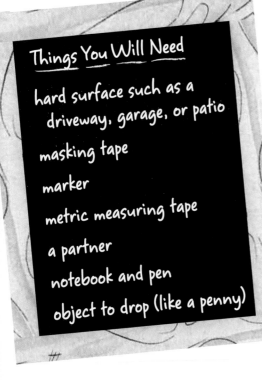

Things You Will Need

hard surface such as a driveway, garage, or patio

masking tape

marker

metric measuring tape

a partner

notebook and pen

object to drop (like a penny)

6

Can you hear it? In your notebook, record whether or not you can hear the penny drop at one meter.

3 Ask your partner to keep dropping the penny at two meters, three meters, and so on. Record the distance each time you hear the penny drop. Where are you when you can no longer hear the penny? Repeat the experiment to get a second set of results.

4 Switch places with your partner and repeat the experiment. Does his or her hearing seem to be the same as yours? Is this what you expected?

How Well Can You Hear Soft Sounds?

An Explanation

When the penny hits a hard surface (the floor), it causes the surface and the air around it to start shaking. This shaking, or vibration, travels through the air to your ear. Inside your ear are an eardrum and other parts that vibrate when sound waves reach them. These vibrating ear parts send a message to your brain, and you hear those vibrations as sound. The closer you are to the vibrations,

FACT: Light travels faster than sound. This means that you can see lightning or fireworks that are far away before you hear the sound they make.

the more sound you will hear. The farther away you are, the less sound you will hear. This is because as sound waves spread out, they get weaker.

 ## Ideas for Your Science Fair

- At what age does human hearing start to lose its strength?

- Is it easier to hear high-pitched sounds or low-pitched sounds?

- What are the best kinds of headphones for blocking outside sounds?

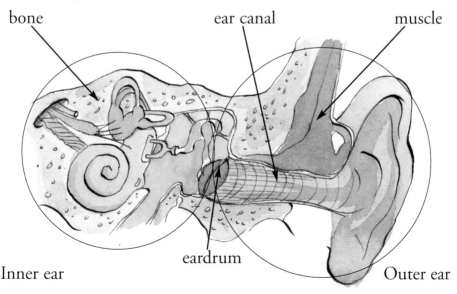

bone   ear canal   muscle

eardrum

Inner ear   Outer ear

Experiment 2
How Do Your Fingers Sense Temperature?

How sensitive are your fingers to different temperatures? Write down your ideas and your reasons for them.

Now Let's Find Out!

1 Fill one foam cup with very warm water from the tap (be sure that it is not scalding). Fill a second foam cup with ice water, and a third cup with room-temperature water. On a table, put the very warm water on your left, the room-temperature water in the center, and the ice water on your right.

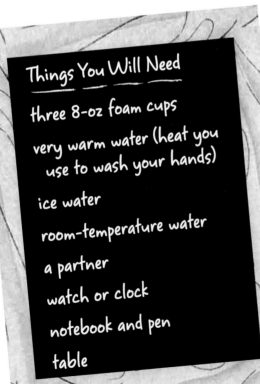

Things You Will Need

three 8-oz foam cups

very warm water (heat you use to wash your hands)

ice water

room-temperature water

a partner

watch or clock

notebook and pen

table

2 Put your right index finger into the warm water and your left index finger into the ice water. What do your

fingers feel? Ask a partner to record your observations in your notebook. What do you think your fingers will feel when you put them into room-temperature water? Why?

3 After two minutes, put both your index fingers into the room-temperature water. What does each of your fingers feel now? Tell your partner to write this in your notebook. Do your fingers feel temperature the way you expected?

4 Try the experiment again, but this time switch the positions of the warm water and ice water. Do your fingers still feel the same when you put them in the room-temperature water? How can you explain this?

How Do Your Fingers Sense Temperature?

An Explanation

When you put a finger into hot water, heat from the water travels into your finger and warms it up. When you put a finger into ice water, heat from your finger travels into the ice water, and that finger cools down.

When you put the "heated up" and "cooled down" fingers into the room-temperature water, the "hot finger"

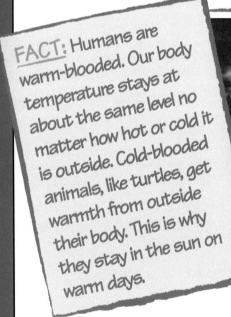

FACT: Humans are warm-blooded. Our body temperature stays at about the same level no matter how hot or cold it is outside. Cold-blooded animals, like turtles, get warmth from outside their body. This is why they stay in the sun on warm days.

loses heat into the water. This makes this finger sense that the room-temperature water is colder than it is. The "cold finger" gains heat from the room-temperature water. This makes this finger sense that the room-temperature water is hotter than it is.

Ideas for Your Science Fair

- Are feet as sensitive to temperature changes as hands?

- Do older people feel cold more quickly than younger people?

- What is the best type of fabric to wrap around a cup of hot water to keep the heat in?

heat flow

cold water   hot water

Experiment 3
How Are Taste and Smell Related?

How does your sense of smell affect your sense of taste? Write down your ideas and your reasons for them.

Now Let's Find Out!

1 You will need to sit at a table for this investigation. Cover your eyes with a blindfold or eye mask.

2 Have your partner feed you a spoonful of each of two flavors of pudding, yogurt, or gelatin while you hold your nose shut. Can you tell which flavor is which?

Things You Will Need

table

blindfold or eye mask

2 spoons

a partner

2 flavors of pudding, yogurt, or gelatin

notebook and pen

3 Now try the taste test without holding your nose. Is it easier this time to tell which flavor you are eating? Why do you think that is? Write down your ideas about smelling and tasting.

4 Clean the spoons. Have your partner wear the blindfold and be the taster, first holding his or her nose. How well can he or she tell which flavor is which?

5 Next, have your partner release his or her nose, and do the taste test once more. Compare your results. Does your sense of taste get better or worse when you can also smell? Which flavor is easier to recognize?

How Are Taste and Smell Related?

An Explanation

Our senses of smell and taste work closely together. About three quarters of what we think is taste really comes from our sense of smell. We can smell something because tiny particles from the object travel to nerve cells in our nose. We also have nerve cells, called taste buds, in our tongue, mouth, and throat that sense taste. The nerve cells in our nose and mouth

FACT: John Harrison has one of the "coolest" jobs in the world. He is the official taste tester for Edy's brand of ice cream. His sense of taste is so important to the company that his tastebuds are insured for one million dollars!

John Harrison, Edy's ice cream taster

work together to send messages to our brain about how something smells and tastes. When you have a cold and cannot smell, it is hard for you to taste your food.

Ideas for Your Science Fair

- Do people lose some of their sense of taste as they get older?

- Do people prefer sweeter foods when they are children more than when they are adults?

- Which parts of your tongue can best pick up sweet tastes? Which can pick up sour tastes?

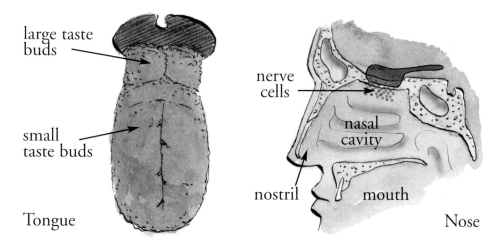

large taste buds

small taste buds

Tongue

nerve cells

nasal cavity

nostril   mouth

Nose

Experiment 4
How Quickly Do Your Nails Grow?

Do your fingernails and toenails grow at the same rate? Write down your ideas and your reasons for them.

Now Let's Find Out!

1 Make a table in your notebook with four columns and at least 20 rows (like in the diagram on the next page). Label the rows and columns as they are in the diagram. (Be sure to include all the rows for your right foot!)

2 First trim all your nails with a nail clipper. Measure each of your fingernails and toenails in millimeters. (Measure from the base of the nail to the tip.) Record each measurement on your table in the "Day 0" column. After 10 days, repeat the measurements and record your results in the table. Remember: DO NOT cut your nails during this experiment!

Things You Will Need

notebook

pencil

nail clipper

metric ruler

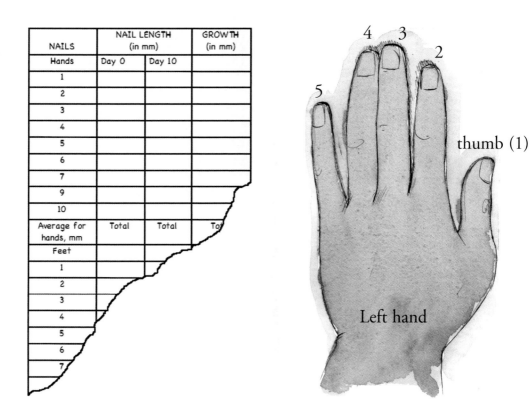

NAILS	NAIL LENGTH (in mm)		GROWTH (in mm)
Hands	Day 0	Day 10	
1			
2			
3			
4			
5			
6			
7			
9			
10			
Average for hands, mm	Total	Total	To
Feet			
1			
2			
3			
4			
5			
6			
7			

thumb (1)

Left hand

3 Subtract the beginning nail length from the final length. This is the amount each nail grew. Record this number in column 4. Now find and record the average growth for your fingernails, and then toenails, after 10 days. Do this by adding all the lengths and dividing them by 10 (the number of nails). Which grew faster, your fingernails or your toenails?

How Quickly Do Your Nails Grow?

An Explanation

For the average person, fingernails grow about 1.5 mm per week. Your toenails, though, grow only half that quickly. Scientists are not sure why this happens. One idea is that your toenails are usually colder than your fingernails. Another is that your fingernails get a better supply of blood than your toenails.

A nail (or plate) is composed of the same material as skin, hair, horn, and hoofs. Nails grow from a root called the nail

FACT: According to the Guinness Book of World Records, the woman who had the longest fingernails was Lee Redmond. Ms. Redmond did not cut her nails from 1979 to 2009. Together, her nails measured 8 m, 65 cm (28 feet, 4.5 inches).

Ms. Redmond, the woman with the longest fingernails

20

matrix. Where the matrix ends, the nail bed begins. The thick base of the nail is called the moon (or lunula). The rest of the nail grows out over the top of the nail bed.

 ## Ideas for Your Science Fair

- Do your nails grow more quickly on your right or left hand?

- Do your fingernails grow more quickly in winter or summer?

- Do your fingernails grow more quickly or slowly as you get older?

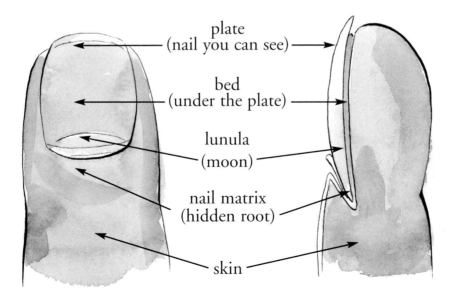

plate
(nail you can see)

bed
(under the plate)

lunula
(moon)

nail matrix
(hidden root)

skin

Experiment 5
How Quick Are Your Reactions?

How quickly can you react to something you see, or hear? Write down your ideas and your reasons for them.

Now Let's Find Out!

1 Stand face-to-face with a partner. Have your partner hold a meterstick toward the top. Line up your finger and thumb exactly at the 50-cm mark on the meterstick. Do not touch the stick, though! Be ready to catch the stick when it is dropped.

2 Ask your partner to drop the measuring stick without telling you first. Try to catch the stick as quickly as you can. At what mark on the stick did you catch it? Write this down. The shorter the distance the stick drops, the quicker your reaction.

Things You Will Need

a partner

meterstick

notebook and pen

22

3 Ask your partner to repeat the stick drop several times. Each time, try to catch the stick as quickly as you can. Do you react more quickly each time?

4 Now close your eyes and have your partner say "Now" as he or she drops the stick. Do this several times. How does your reaction compare?

5 Change places so that you are dropping the stick for your partner. Who has faster reactions, you or your partner? Are your reaction times different for sight and sound?

How Quick Are Your Reactions?
An Explanation

People react at different speeds to things happening around them. In sports, like baseball and racing, the athletes need to have very fast reactions. Ballplayers might need to make a tough catch, and track athletes need to react quickly to the starting gun. When you saw your partner drop the meterstick or heard your partner say "Now," you needed to

FACT: Most humans react more quickly to sounds than sights. This is because sound takes less time to reach the brain than sights do. When we are startled, by sound or sight, our faces show surprise!

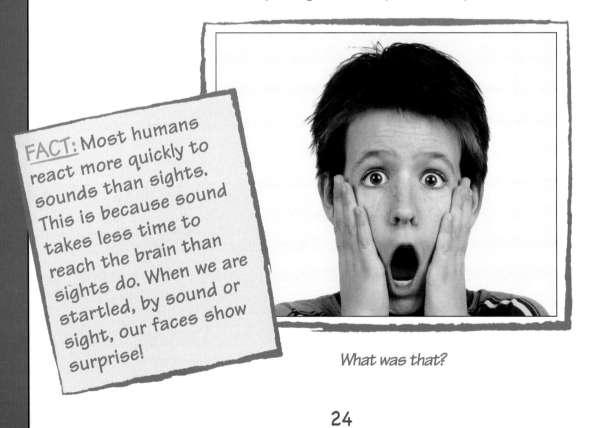

What was that?

react very quickly to catch the stick before it hit the ground. The more practice you had in catching the stick, the quicker your reactions.

 ## Ideas for Your Science Fair

- Do older people have slower reaction times than younger people?

- If you are right-handed, will your catching reaction be slower with your left hand?

- Do your reactions get slower if you are tired?

Experiment 6
Which Eye Color Is Most Common?

In a group of your friends, which eye color do you think is the most common? Write down your ideas and your reasons for them.

Now Let's Find Out!

1 Make a table for recording different eye colors. Along the top, draw and label blue, brown, gray, hazel, and green eyes. Leave room for any other eye colors you may observe.

2 Write all your friends' names in the left column. In the last row, write "Total."

Things You Will Need

10 to 15 friends

pencil and paper

coloring pens

3 Look closely at the eyes of your friends. Mark each person's eye color against his or her name.

EYE CHART

Color → / Name ↓	Blue	Brown	Hazel	Gray	Green	Other
Mitch	X					
Latisha		X				
Maria		X				
Trevor					X	
Pedro		X				
Karen	X					
Total	2	3	0	0	1	0

4 Count how many friends have each kind of eye color. Write the number in the Total row of your table. How many of your friends have blue eyes? Brown eyes? What other eye colors did you observe?

5 What was the most common color of eyes among your friends? Do you think it would be similar for other groups of friends?

Which Eye Color Is Most Common?

An Explanation

You get your eye color from your parents. The most common eye color in the world is brown. The least common eye color is green.

Eye colors in humans can vary from the very darkest brown to the very lightest blue. Eye color depends on the

FACT: Scientists in Denmark have discovered that all blue-eyed people in the world can be traced back to one person. This person lived between 6,000 and 10,000 years ago. He or she was able to pass this trait to his or her children. Prior to this, all humans had brown eyes!

Blue eyes

28

amount of three kinds of pigments in the eye's iris (the colored part). These pigments are brown, yellow, and blue.

 ## Ideas for Your Science Fair

- What eye color is most common in your family?
- What natural hair colors are most common with blue eyes?
- How can you enlarge your pupils (the black center of your eye)?

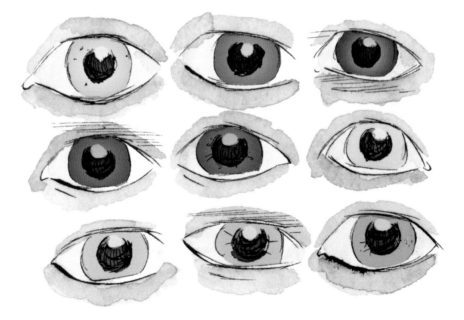

Do Both Your Eyes See the Same?

How does your vision change from one eye to the other? Write down your ideas and your reasons for them.

Now Let's Find Out!

1   To see which of your eyes you favor, overlap your hands and leave an open triangle between them. The base of the triangle is your crossed thumbs.

2   Hold your overlapped hands at arm's length. Look through the triangle between your hands at an object about 1 meter (3 feet) away from you. Center the object in the triangle.

Things You Will Need

5 people
pencil and paper

3   As you look at the object, close one eye. Then open it and close the other eye. The eye that sees the object through the

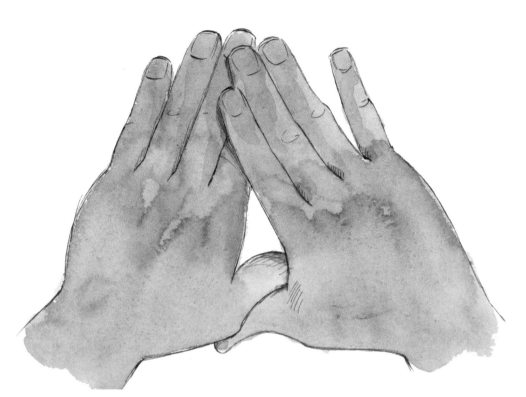

Make a see-through triangle with your hands.

triangle will be the eye you favor. Record which eye this is. Repeat the eye test with five other people. Record your results.

4 Which eye did most people favor? Try looking at the object and moving your hands toward the eye you do NOT favor. What happens to the object?

Do Both Your Eyes See the Same?
An Explanation

People can prefer, or favor, one eye over the other. They can also favor both eyes equally. Most people (about two-thirds) favor their right eye over their left. Your brain controls which eye you favor, but scientists are not quite sure exactly why this happens. People also can favor one ear over the other, as well as one hand, foot, and side of face.

FACT: Some scientists say that people favor one side of their face over the other when making expressions. They say that many people show their feelings with the left side of their face. They show more about their thoughts with the right.

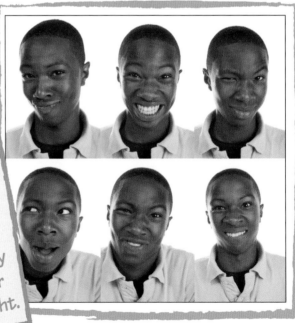

Ideas for Your Science Fair

- Do right-handed people favor their right eye and left-handed people their left eye?

- If people wear glasses, do they still favor one eye over the other?

- Is the favored eye the same one that people use when aiming a paper airplane?

How Are Fingerprints Similar and Different?

In what ways are your fingerprints similar to and different from other people's? Write down your ideas and your reasons for them.

Now Let's Find Out!

1 Make fingerprint cards for you and a partner. Put one finger at a time on an ink pad, then lightly roll it left to right onto an index card. Write your name on the card and label your fingerprints. Do the same for your partner. When you finish, wash your hands.

Things You Will Need

a partner
black ink pad (water-based)
plain white index cards
magnifying glass
soap and water
pen and pencil

2 Compare your fingerprints to the pictures of the main fingerprint patterns. Do you have mostly arches, loops, or whorls in your fingerprints?

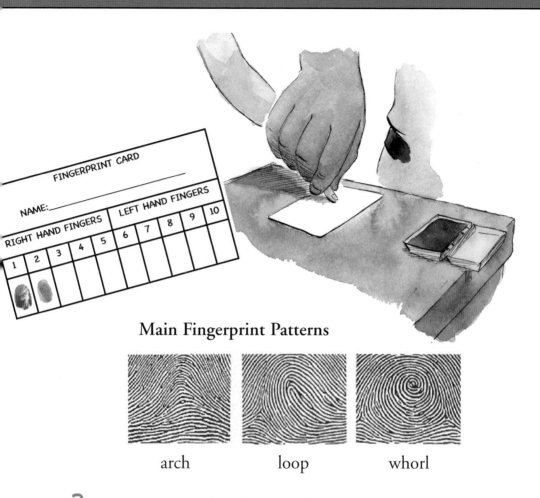

Main Fingerprint Patterns

arch   loop   whorl

3 Compare each of your fingerprints to the others. How are they alike and how are they different?

4 Study the prints on both cards with a magnifying glass. In what ways are your partner's prints the same as and different from yours? Can you find any prints that look similar, or the same?

How Are Fingerprints Similar and Different?

An Explanation

Human fingerprints are the patterns of skin on the finger pads. Prints of the pads are left on some surfaces when the pads touch that surface. Although they can have similar patterns such as arches, loops, and whorls, each fingerprint is one of a kind.

No two people have exactly the same fingerprints. This

FACT: Author Mark Twain was one of the first to write about using fingerprints to solve mysteries. In 1894, he wrote about using them in his book The Tragedy of Pudd'nhead Wilson. In 1897, the first fingerprint office opened in India.

Mark Twain

is why fingerprints are taken and used in crime investigations. They can prove that a certain person was present at the crime scene. They are often left on things we hold, like drink glasses, and can be seen better using a magnifying glass.

 ## Ideas for Your Science Fair

- How similar are your fingerprints to those of your parents? Your grandparents?

- How do the prints from your toes compare to the ones on your fingers?

- Which fingerprint pattern is most common in a group of ten friends?

How Does Exercise Affect Your Heart Rate?

What happens to the speed of your heart when you exercise? Write down your ideas and your reasons for them.

Now Let's Find Out!

1 Sit in a comfortable chair for ten minutes. Then ask a partner to take your pulse for one minute. To do this, he or she should put two fingers on the inside of your wrist, below your thumb. Once your partner finds your pulse, he or she should count the number of beats for one minute. Write this number in your notebook. It is your "resting heart rate."

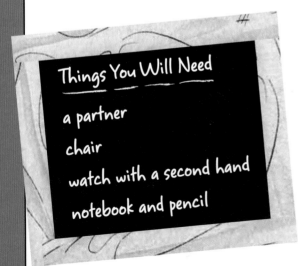

Things You Will Need

a partner

chair

watch with a second hand

notebook and pencil

2 Do thirty jumping jacks in a safe, open space. When you finish, ask your partner to take your pulse for one minute. Write this down as your "exercise heart rate."

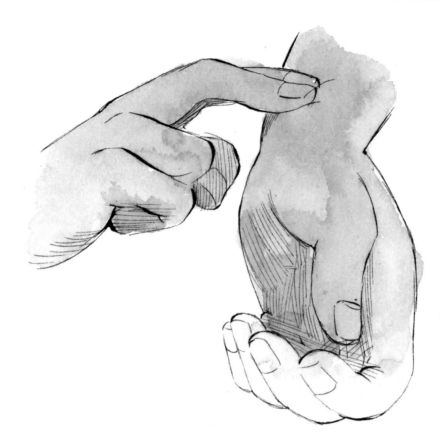

3 Next, have your partner take your pulse five minutes after you finish your jumping jacks. Is it back to the "resting rate" yet? How long does it take your heart to get back to its resting rate?

4 Switch places and do exactly the same with your partner's pulse. How long does it take your partner's heart to get back to its resting rate? Which of you recovered more quickly?

How Does Exercise Affect Your Heart Rate?

An Explanation

Your heart works as a pump to move blood through your body. When you are resting, your heart beats at a resting rate. For children 1 to 10 years old, the range for a resting rate is between 70 and 140 beats per minute.

When you exercise, your muscles need more oxygen-filled blood. Your heart beats more quickly to get the

FACT: You can lower your resting heart rate with exercise. Your heart muscle can become thicker and pump more blood with each beat. Some athletes have heart rates as low as 35 to 50 beats per minute!

oxygen to your muscles. After you exercise, it takes time for your heart rate to get back to normal. The more physically fit you are, the more quickly this happens.

 ## Ideas for Your Science Fair

- How does daily exercise (jumping jacks for 10 minutes) affect your resting heart rate?

- How does exercise change your breathing rate?

- How does your heart rate change when you watch exciting events?

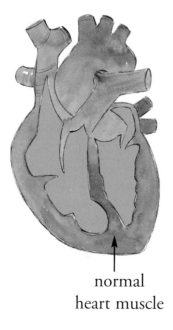

normal
heart muscle

athlete's heart with
thicker heart muscle

How Are Strands of Hair the Same and Different?

In what ways are pieces of human hair the same and different? Write down your ideas and your reasons for them.

Now Let's Find Out!

1 Collect hair from the heads of five people. Tape the ends of each of the hairs onto a sheet of drawing paper. Write the name and age of the person who gave you the hair above each sample.

Things You Will Need

safety scissors
5 people of different ages
(try to include a person
with gray or white hair)
clear tape
plain white drawing paper
notebook and pen
magnifying glass

2 Look closely at each hair with your magnifier, especially at the ends of the hairs. Write the color of each hair in your notebook next to the person's name. Also write whether the hair is straight, wavy, or curly.

3 Can you tell if some of the hairs are thicker than others? Run each of the samples through your fingers. Do they all feel the same? In what ways are all the hairs alike? Write your observations in your notebook.

4 In what ways are the hairs different? If you have a white or gray hair to observe, how is it different from the other hairs? Write down these observations as well.

How Are Strands of Hair the Same and Different?

An Explanation

Humans have hair growing just about all over their bodies. Hair is a protein that grows out of follicles in the skin. Each follicle can make around twenty hairs in a person's lifetime.

Hair can be different colors and thicknesses. Colors can include black, brown, red, sandy, yellow (blond), gray, and white. There are also many different hair types. These types

FACT: Most people with a full head of hair have around 100,000 hairs on their head. People with blond hair have more hairs on their heads than people with black hair, but black hairs are thicker. People with red hair have the fewest number of hairs on their head.

include fine, medium, coarse, and wiry, depending on the thickness of each strand. A whole "head of hair" can be thin, medium, or thick and also be straight, curly, tightly coiled, or wavy. Gray hair is usually more coarse than non-gray hair.

 ## Ideas for Your Science Fair

- What does conditioner do for hair?

- Does hair feel different after it is washed in hot water than after it is washed in cool water?

- How does a human hair compare with a cat's or a dog's hair?

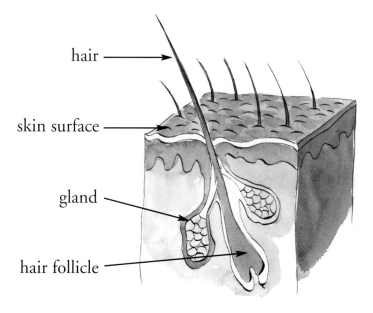

hair ——→

skin surface ——→

gland ——→

hair follicle ——→

Words to Know

cells—The smallest units of life.

eardrum—Part of the ear that vibrates with sound.

follicle—Tiny part of the skin where hair grows.

nerve cells—Cells that send messages back and forth between the body, the brain, and the spinal cord.

oxygen—A gas that many living things need to survive.

particles—Tiny bits of a material.

pattern—Something that repeats in a predictable way.

pigments—Color-containing chemicals.

pulse—Heartbeat felt on the outside of the body.

range—In mathematics, the highest and lowest numbers in a set of numbers.

reactions—Ways your body responds when something happens.

taste buds—Special cells in the mouth that sense tastes.

temperature—A measure of how hot something is.

trait—A feature inherited from parents.

vibration—A shaking motion.

Learn More

Books

Murphy, Pat, Ellen Macaulay, and the Staff of the Exploratorium. *Exploratopia*. New York: Little, Brown, 2006.

Simon, Seymour. *Eyes and Ears*. New York: Harper Collins, 2005.

Smith, Penny, ed. *First Human Body Encyclopedia*. New York: DK Publishing, 2005.

VanCleave, Janice. *Great Science Project Ideas from Real Kids*. New York: Sterling Publishing Co., Inc., 2006.

Internet Addresses

Kids.gov. *Health and Safety*.
http://www.kids.gov/k_5/k_5_health_issues.shtml

Kids' Health.
http://www.kidshealth.org/kid/

National Geographic. *Explore the Human Body*.
http://science.nationalgeographic.com/science/health-and-human-body/human-body

Index